COUNTRY  PROFILES

FRANCE

BY AMY RECHNER

BLASTOFF!
DISCOVERY

BELLWETHER MEDIA • MINNEAPOLIS, MN

Blastoff! Discovery launches
a new mission: reading to learn.
Filled with facts and features, each
book offers you an exciting new
world to explore!

This edition first published in 2018 by Bellwether Media, Inc.

No part of this publication may be reproduced in whole or in
part without written permission of the publisher.
For information regarding permission, write to Bellwether
Media, Inc., Attention: Permissions Department,
5357 Penn Avenue South, Minneapolis, MN 55419.

Library of Congress Cataloging-in-Publication Data

Names: Rechner, Amy, author.
Title: France / by Amy Rechner.
Description: Minneapolis, MN : Bellwether Media, Inc., 2018.
    | Series: Blastoff! Discovery: Country Profiles | Includes
    bibliographical references and index. | Audience: Grades
    3-8. | Audience: Ages 7-13.
Identifiers: LCCN 2016055085 (print) |
    LCCN 2016057125 (ebook) | ISBN 9781626176805
    (hardcover : alkaline paper) | ISBN 9781681034102
    (ebook)
Subjects: LCSH: France–Juvenile literature.
Classification: LCC DC17 .R43 2018 (print) | LCC DC17
    (ebook) | DDC 944–dc23
LC record available at https://lccn.loc.gov/2016055085

Editor: Christina Leaf   Designer: Brittany McIntosh

Printed in the United States of America, North Mankato, MN.

TABLE OF CONTENTS

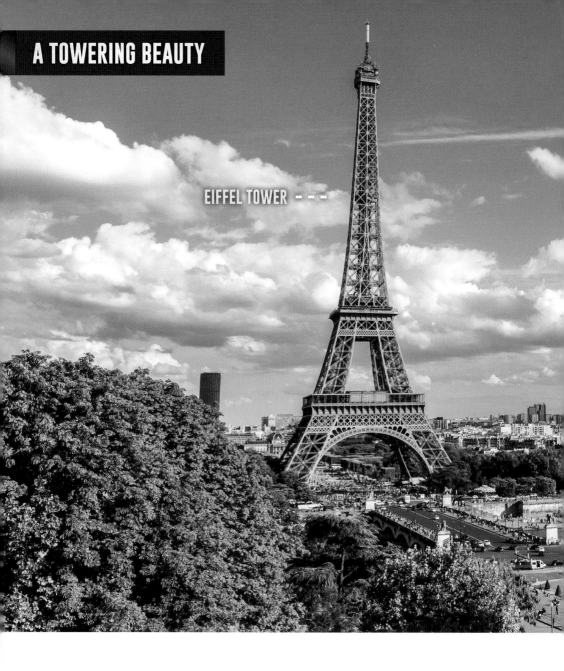

EIFFEL TOWER - - -

A family of **tourists** wanders the streets of Paris. Everywhere they go, the Eiffel Tower is visible in the distance. When it first opened in 1889, the people of Paris thought it was ugly. Now it is a world-famous **landmark**.

OTHER TOP SITES

FRENCH RIVIERA

LOUVRE MUSEUM

MONT SAINT-MICHEL

VERSAILLES

The Eiffel Tower stands 1,063 feet (324 meters) high. The family zips up to the top in an elevator. From the top, the city of Paris is spread out at their feet. Historic landmarks like the Arc de Triomphe stand proudly amid the buildings and traffic of a modern city. This is France!

France is the largest country in Western Europe, covering 212,935 square miles (551,500 square kilometers). The capital city, Paris, is in north-central France. The Bay of Biscay is to France's west. The English Channel borders France to the northwest, and to the northeast are Belgium and Luxembourg. Germany, Switzerland, and Italy line the eastern border. Spain, Andorra, and the Mediterranean Sea are south.

The island of Corsica, in the Mediterranean Sea, is also part of France. Along France's southern coast, the tiny country of Monaco occupies less than 1 square mile (2.6 square kilometers) of land.

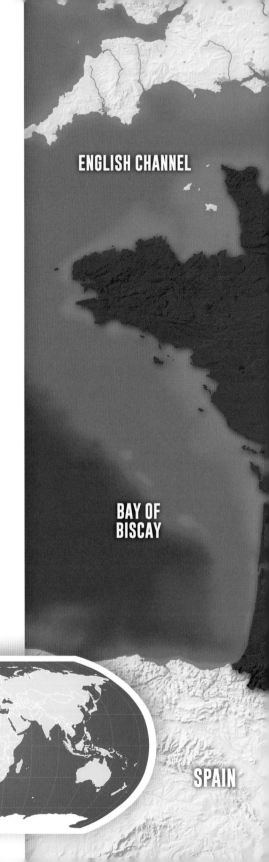

ENGLISH CHANNEL

BAY OF BISCAY

SPAIN

BELGIUM

NOT JUST IN EUROPE

Five overseas territories are also
considered part of France. One is in
South America. Two are islands in the
Caribbean Sea, and two are islands
near southern Africa.

PARIS

LUXEMBOURG

GERMANY

FRANCE

SWITZERLAND

LYON

ITALY

TOULOUSE

MARSEILLE

NICE - - - MONACO

ANDORRA

MEDITERRANEAN
SEA

CORSICA

Central France is covered in flat **plains** and rolling hills. The Seine and Loire Rivers flow northwest through its countryside and cities. Along the Spanish border rise the Pyrenees Mountains. The Alps mountain range looms along the eastern border. At 15,771 feet (4,807 meters), the Alps' Mont Blanc is the highest point in France.

SEINE RIVER

LOIRE RIVER

◼ = PYRENEES   ◼ = FRENCH ALPS

LOIRE RIVER

BLOW THE MAN DOWN

A strong, cold wind called a *mistral* blows across southern France in late winter. It comes from the north and can get as strong as 81 miles (130 kilometers) per hour as it nears the coast.

FRENCH ALPS

PARIS
Average seasonal highs and lows

JANUARY
HIGH: 46 °F (8 °C)
LOW: 37 °F (3 °C)

APRIL
HIGH: 59 °F (15 °C)
LOW: 43 °F (6 °C)

JULY
HIGH: 77 °F (25 °C)
LOW: 59 °F (15 °C)

OCTOBER
HIGH: 63 °F (17 °C)
LOW: 48 °F (9 °C)

°F = degrees Fahrenheit
°C = degrees Celsius

In northern France, the weather moves quickly. Clouds and rain appear almost daily. Weather in central and northeastern France features cold, snowy winters and warm summers. Deep snow buries the Alps and the Pyrenees in winter. Southern France enjoys mild winters and hot, dry summers.

WILDLIFE

France's mountains are home to a variety of wildlife that includes lynx, brown bears, and ibex. Chamois, animals similar to goats and antelopes, prosper in the alpine woodlands alongside mountain hares. Deer and wild boar roam the countryside.

Many birds live along France's Mediterranean coast. Some of them, like the Egyptian vulture, stop over as they **migrate** from Africa. Hawks and falcons swoop down from rocky cliffs. White storks live in the Alsace region near Germany. There are flamingos, heron, and egrets in a **nature reserve** called the Camargue.

- - - EGYPTIAN
VULTURE

EURASIAN LYNX

WILD BOAR

MOUNTAIN HARE

WHITE STORK

10

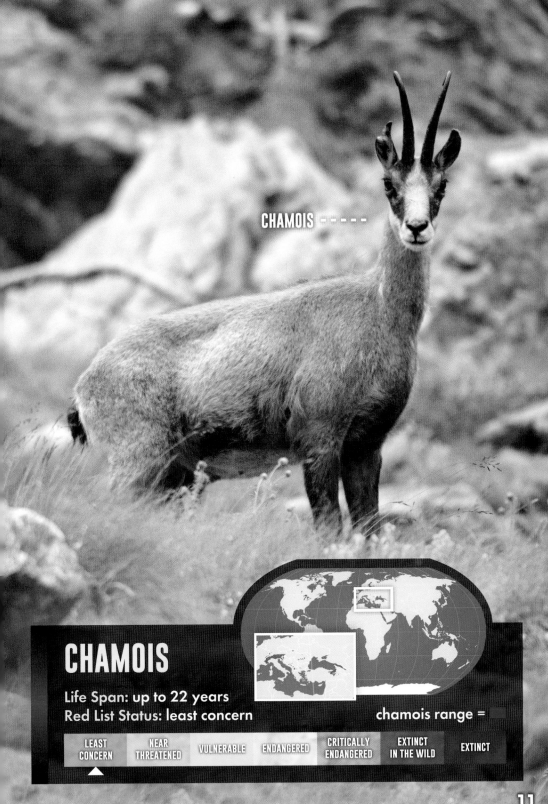

CHAMOIS - - - - -

CHAMOIS

Life Span: up to 22 years
Red List Status: least concern

chamois range =

LEAST CONCERN	NEAR THREATENED	VULNERABLE	ENDANGERED	CRITICALLY ENDANGERED	EXTINCT IN THE WILD	EXTINCT

There are nearly 63 million people in **mainland** France. The population is very **diverse**. In addition to people from the French-owned islands, many **immigrants** come from North Africa, the **Middle East**, and other European countries. The national language is French, but local **accents** can sound very different.

France does not have a national religion, although many French people are Catholic. The country is also home to 5 million Muslims and the largest Jewish population in Western Europe. Nearly one-quarter of French people do not follow any religion.

FAMOUS FACE

Name: **Napoleon Bonaparte**
Birthday: **August 15, 1769**
Hometown: **Ajaccio, France**
Famous for: **French military leader and emperor who conquered much of Europe in the early 19th century**

SPEAK FRENCH

ENGLISH	FRENCH	HOW TO SAY IT
hello	bonjour	bon-ZHOOR
goodbye	au revoir	oh ruh-VWAH
please	s'il vous plaît	seel voo PLAY
thank you	merci	mehr-SEE
yes	oui	we
no	non	noh

AIX-EN-PROVENCE

TRAM, NICE

Most French people live in or near large cities. In old cities like Paris and Marseille, families often live in apartments. Many buildings are hundreds of years old. Single-family homes are more common in **suburbs**. The **rural** populations in France are small. Trains connect France's cities and towns. In Paris, people walk, drive, or use the *Métro* subway system.

French families are small, but extended families often live near each other. Spending time with family is very important in France. French children may help with shopping and other tasks.

IN THE BAG

French groceries generally do not require a shopping cart. People buy just what they need for a day or two and carry it home in reusable bags. Different shops sell fresh meat, vegetables, bread, and other foods.

The people of France are very proud of their country and **heritage**. They are glad to talk to visitors, especially those who try to speak their language. When treated with respect, the French are very friendly and welcoming people. They greet strangers and new friends with a firm handshake. Friends and family exchange kisses on each cheek.

CAFE, PARIS

French people have great enthusiasm for life. They enjoy beauty in scenery, fashion, and art. They value good food and good company, and they love to talk and argue ideas.

French children must attend school from ages 6 to 16. Most attend public schools, although private schools are also an option. After middle school, or *collège*, most students attend high school, or *lycée*, to prepare for university. Some train for trade or technical jobs.

France is the most visited country in the world. Many French people work in tourism jobs at hotels and restaurants. Others work in different **service jobs** such as in shops or banks. French factory workers manufacture automobiles, chemicals, and aircraft. Farmers produce grains and livestock, while **vineyard** workers harvest grapes to make wine.

GROCER

VINEYARD WORKER

SOCCER

Soccer, or *le football*, is the most popular sport in France. People play in leagues and cheer for the national team. Rugby and tennis are popular, too. The Tour de France, a famous bike race, challenges world-class cyclists and thrills spectators. Hikers enjoy trails that wind along mountains, plains, and coastlines. In winter, resorts in the French Alps fill with skiers.

TOUR DE FRANCE

The French have other favorite activities as well. People enjoy talking, reading, eating, and watching movies. Live music, art museums, and dance performances are an important part of French culture, too. Opinions about the arts make a great topic of conversation!

TAKE A BREAK

Vacation and family time are very important in France. Workers get at least a month of vacation each year. They are also known for only working 35 hours each week, rather than the more common 40 hours.

ESCARGOT

This game is like hopscotch, except in a spiral shape like a snail's shell. *Escargot* is the French word for snail.

How to Play:
1. Draw a spiral on the sidewalk with chalk. Divide it into at least 15 numbered squares.

2. On one foot, jump on each square to the middle spot, which is a resting spot.

3. Jump on one foot on all squares to get back.

4. If a player steps on a line, they are out.

5. If a player makes it all the way in and back, they can place their initials or a rock on any square. Opponents have to skip that square.

6. The game ends when it is impossible to jump into the center space. The player who owns the most squares wins!

DAILY BREAD

The long, skinny loaf of French bread is called a *baguette*. Baguettes are purchased fresh every day to be served with lunch and dinner. Leftover baguettes make morning toast.

French people take both food and the act of eating very seriously. They allow plenty of time for meals so they can savor the food as well as the company. Even lunchtime can be two hours long!

France is famous for its **cuisine**. Portions are usually small and carefully prepared. Fresh bread accompanies most meals, starting with buttery croissants for breakfast. Lunch or dinner might start with soup. One favorite is onion soup topped with melted cheese. Fish or meat comes next, followed by a cheese plate or dessert. Delicate, folded pancakes called *crêpes* can be filled with vegetables for dinner or chocolate for dessert.

CROISSANTS

ONION SOUP

CRÊPES

CROQUES MONSIEUR RECIPE

Ingredients:
1 tablespoon softened butter
2 slices of bread
2 slices of ham
1 slice Swiss or Gruyère cheese

Steps:
1. Preheat the oven to 350 degrees Fahrenheit (180 degrees Celsius).

2. Spread the butter on one side of each piece of bread.

3. Cover the unbuttered side of a slice with ham. Trim off any extra ham and place it in the middle.

4. Place the sliced cheese over the ham.

5. Put the other slice of bread on top, butter side facing out. Put the sandwich on an ovenproof plate.

6. With an adult, bake the sandwich in the oven for about 15 minutes. Flip it over halfway through. Be sure to wear oven mitts to take it out of the oven. *Bon appétit!*

France has many national holidays. Some are based on Christian holidays, like Easter. On this day, stories say that flying church bells ring and scatter Easter chocolates for children to find. Christmas and Mardi Gras are also exciting events.

The biggest national holiday is Bastille Day on July 14. It honors the French **Republic**. A huge military parade and fireworks light up Paris. Each June 21, the whole country bursts into song with the *Fête de la Musique*. Free music performances are held across the country. Taking time to enjoy the good things in life is what France is all about!

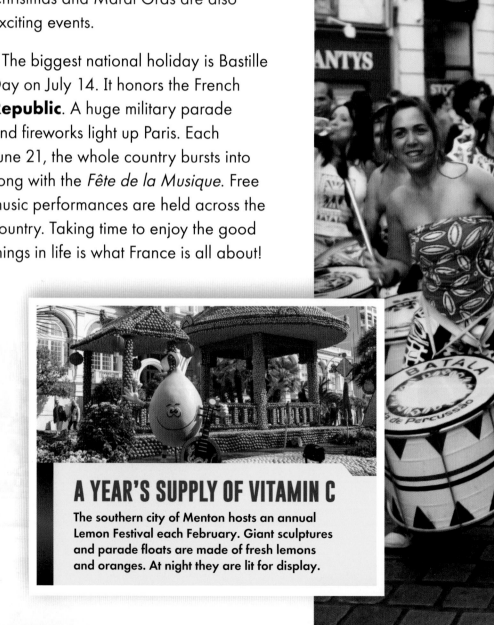

A YEAR'S SUPPLY OF VITAMIN C

The southern city of Menton hosts an annual Lemon Festival each February. Giant sculptures and parade floats are made of fresh lemons and oranges. At night they are lit for display.

1429

Joan of Arc leads French troops against the English during the Hundred Years War

51 BCE

Julius Caesar conquers Gaul, the ancient name for France

1789

Angry French citizens storm Paris's Bastille prison and start the French Revolution

800 CE

Charlemagne becomes emperor of the Holy Roman Empire, which includes France

1643

Louis XIV, known as the Sun King, begins his 72-year reign

1914-1918
Many battles occur on French soil as France fights Germany in World War I

1958
France adopts a new constitution

1793
King Louis XVI and Queen Marie-Antoinette are overthrown

1993
France joins the European Union

1940
Germany begins a four-year occupation of France during World War II

1804
Napoleon Bonaparte names himself Emperor of France

2007
Newly-elected president Nicolas Sarkozy chooses women to fill half of the positions in his cabinet to bring diversity to government roles

FRANCE FACTS

Official Name: French Republic

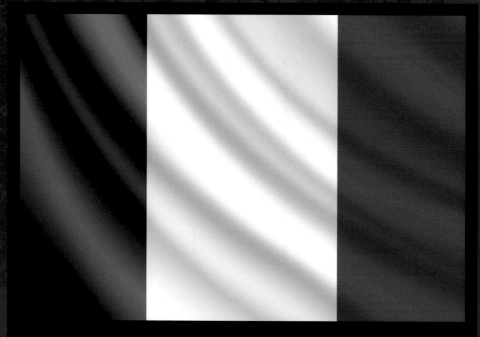

Flag of France: The tricolor design of vertical stripes in blue, white, and red was adopted in 1794. The three colors signify the three main principles of the Revolution, which were liberty, equality, and brotherhood.

Area: 212,935 square miles
   (551,500 square kilometers)

Capital City: Paris

Important Cities: Toulouse, Marseille, Lyon, Nice

Population:

62,814,233 in mainland France (July 2016)

COUNTRYSIDE
20.5%

WHERE PEOPLE LIVE

CITY
79.5%

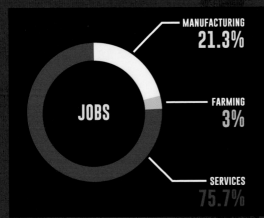

MANUFACTURING
21.3%

JOBS

FARMING
3%

SERVICES
75.7%

Main Exports:

machinery

aircraft

chemicals

medications

plastics

beverages

National Holiday:
Bastille Day (July 14)

Main Language:
French

Form of Government:
semi-presidential republic

Title for Country Leaders:
president, prime minister

RELIGION

NONE
25%

OTHER
3%

MUSLIM
8%

CHRISTIAN
64%

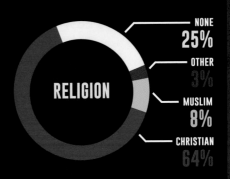

Unit of Money:
Euro; 100 cents equal one Euro.

GLOSSARY

accents—different ways to pronounce a language's words, based on location

cuisine—a style of cooking

diverse—made up of people or things that are different from one another

heritage—the traditions, achievements, and beliefs that are part of the history of a group of people

immigrants—people who move to a new country

landmark—an important structure or place

mainland—the main part of a continent or country

Middle East—a region of southwestern Asia and northern Africa; this region includes Egypt, Lebanon, Iran, Iraq, Israel, Saudi Arabia, Syria, and other nearby countries.

migrate—to travel from one place to another, often with the seasons

nature reserve—an area where animals and other natural resources are protected

plains—large areas of flat land

republic—a government in which citizens choose the leader through voting

rural—related to the countryside

service jobs—jobs that perform tasks for people or businesses

suburbs—towns and communities just outside of a large city

tourists—people who travel to visit another place

vineyard—a field of grapevines

TO LEARN MORE

AT THE LIBRARY

Greathead, Helen. *City Trails: Paris*. Oakland, Calif.: Lonely Planet, 2016.

Peppas, Lynn. *Cultural Traditions in France*. New York, N.Y.: Crabtree Publishing, 2014.

Sonneborn, Liz. *France*. New York, N.Y.: Scholastic Children's Press, 2013.

ON THE WEB

Learning more about France is as easy as 1, 2, 3.

1. Go to www.factsurfer.com.

2. Enter "France" into the search box.

3. Click the "Surf" button and you will see a list of related web sites.

With factsurfer.com, finding more information is just a click away.

INDEX